Duden

kurz geübt & schnell kapiert

Englischheft
6. Klasse

Dudenverlag
Berlin

Lernplan von _____

1	Seite	**Wortarten: Adjektiv und Adverb**	bearbeiten am	☹ 😐 🙂	↺ ✓
	4	Adjektive – Steigerung (1)		🙂	
	6	Adjektive – Steigerung (2)		🙂	
	8	Adjektive – Steigerung: alle Formen		🙂	
	10	Adverbien		🙂	
2	Seite	**Wortarten: Pronomen und Mengenangaben**	bearbeiten am	☹ 😐 🙂	↺ ✓
	12	Mengenangaben: some und any		🙂	
	14	Zusammensetzungen mit some / any		🙂	
3	Seite	**Wortarten: Präpositionen und Zahlen**	bearbeiten am	☹ 😐 🙂	↺ ✓
	16	Präpositionen des Ortes		🙂	
	18	Präpositionen der Zeit		🙂	
4	Seite	**Die Zeitformen des Verbs**	bearbeiten am	☹ 😐 🙂	↺ ✓
	20	Modale Hilfsverben		🙂	
	22	simple past – Aussagesätze		🙂	
	24	simple past – Fragesätze		🙂	
	26	simple past – Aussagen, Verneinungen, Fragen		🙂	
	28	Vermischte Übungen		🙂	

Seite	Die Zeitformen des Verbs	bearbeiten am	☹ 😐 🙂	↺ ✓
38	simple present und simple past (1)		😐	
40	simple present und simple past (2)		😐	
42	will-future		😐	
44	going to-future		😐	
46	will-future und going to-future		😐	
48	present perfect – Aussagesätze		😐	
50	present perfect – Verneinungen		😐	
52	present perfect – Fragesätze		😐	
54	present perfect und simple past		😐	
56	mixed tenses		😐	
58	mixed tenses – Fragen		😐	

5	Seite	Der Satz	bearbeiten am	☹ 😐 🙂	↺ ✓
	60	Wortstellung		😐	
	62	Vermischte Übungen		😐	
	29	**Lösungen**			

Adjektive – Steigerung (1)

Adjektive (*adjectives*) beschreiben Personen und Sachen, z. B.:
Here you see a **careful** driver with a **fantastic** car.
  adjective   *adjective*

Wenn man Personen oder Sachen miteinander **vergleichen** will, kann man **Adjektive steigern**.
Einsilbige Adjektive und Adjektive mit der Endung -y steigert man, indem man **-er** und **-est** anhängt, z. B.:

Adjektiv	Komparativ	Superlativ
big	bigg**er**	bigg**est**
noisy	nois**ier**	nois**iest**

Es gibt aber einige **Ausnahmen**, die unregelmäßig gesteigert werden, z. B.:

Adjektiv	Komparativ	Superlativ
good	better	best
bad	worse	worst
much	more	most

1 In der folgenden Tabelle erhältst du Informationen über eine Stadt *(city)*, eine Kleinstadt *(town)* und ein Dorf *(village)*. Vergleiche die drei miteinander. Benutze zum Vergleichen die Adjektive in den Klammern und schreibe jeweils einen Satz.
Tipp: Vergiss beim Komparativ nicht, *than* zu verwenden.

	city	town	village
size	big	mid-sized*	small
streets	dirty	clean	very clean
loudness	noisy	quiet	very quiet
traffic	busy	not so busy	quiet
bus service	good	not so good	bad
inhabitants**	300,000	50,000	250

* *mid-sized* = mittelgroß
** *inhabitants* = Einwohner

1 **Wortarten: Adjektiv und Adverb**

1. village (clean) town *The village is cleaner than the town.*
2. town (clean) city _____
3. village (small) town _____
4. city (big) town _____
5. town (dirty) village _____
6. town (small) city _____
7. village (quiet) town _____
8. town (big) village _____
9. city (noisy) town _____
10. town (quiet) city _____
11. city (busy) town _____ | 10 |

2 Ergänze die folgenden Sätze mit den richtigen Formen von *good*, *bad*, *big* und *small*.

1. The bus service in the city is _____ than the bus service in the town.
2. The bus service in the village is _____ than the bus service in the town.
3. The city is the _____ place of the three.
4. The village is the _____ place of the three. | 4 |

Adjektive – Steigerung (2)

Alle Adjektive, die drei und mehr Silben haben oder die zwei Silben haben und nicht auf -y enden, steigert man mit **more/most** und **less/least**, z. B.:

Grundform	*expensive*	teuer
Komparativ	*more expensive*	teurer
Superlativ	*most expensive*	am teuersten
Komparativ	*less expensive*	nicht so teuer, billiger
Superlativ	*least expensive*	am wenigsten teuer

Grundform	*famous*	berühmt
Komparativ	*more famous*	berühmter
Superlativ	*most famous*	am berühmtesten
Komparativ	*less famous*	weniger berühmt
Superlativ	*least famous*	am wenigsten berühmt

❶ Vergleiche die Fahrzeuge und benutze dabei die Adjektive in Klammern.

Mr Brown wants to buy a new car for his family. You can see four different cars here. He compares the prices and the engines*.

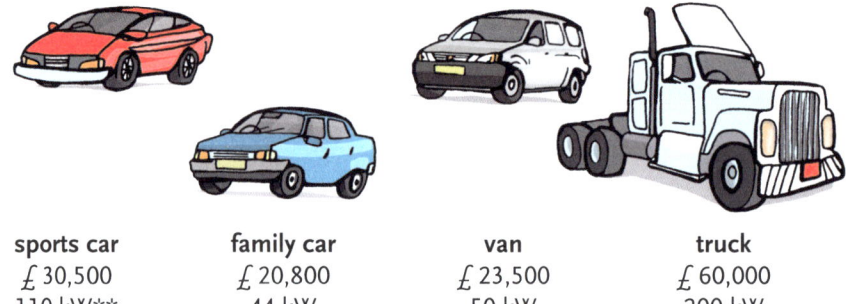

sports car	family car	van	truck
£ 30,500	£ 20,800	£ 23,500	£ 60,000
110 kW**	44 kW	50 kW	200 kW

* engine = Motor
** kW = Kilowatt

1 Wortarten: Adjektiv und Adverb

1. the sports car (expensive) the family car <u>The sports car is more expensive than the family car. / The family car is less expensive than the sports car.</u>

2. the truck (powerful) the van _____

3. the van (powerful) the family car _____

4. the family car (useful) the sports car _____

5. the sports car (expensive) the van _____

6. the truck (expensive) <u>The truck is the</u> _____ car. ☐ 5

★ **2** Mr Brown will sich zwischen dem Sport- und Familienauto entscheiden. Schreibe auf, was er über die beiden Autos denkt. Benutze die Adjektive in Klammern.

1. the sports car (small) <u>The sports car is the smallest car</u>.

2. the family car (comfortable) the sports car _____

3. the family car (useful) the sports car _____ <u>for a family</u>.

4. the sports car (beautiful) _____ <u>car</u>.

5. the family car (good) _____ <u>for me</u>. ☐ 4

7

Adjektive – Steigerung: alle Formen

1 In der Tabelle stehen sechs Adjektive. Schreibe zu jedem Adjektiv den Komparativ und den Superlativ auf.

Adjektiv	Komparativ	Superlativ
nice		
short		
big	*bigger*	
easy		
famous		*most famous*
dangerous		

1 Wortarten: Adjektiv und Adverb

2 Schreibe jedes der folgenden Adjektive unter dasjenige Adjektiv in der Tabelle (s. Aufgabe 1), das auf die gleiche Weise gesteigert wird. Bilde dann die Komparative und die Superlative.

beautiful   red   loud   wide   heavy   hot   silly
fine   nervous   old   intelligent   useful

| 36 |

3 Ben und Sarah gehen zum ersten Mal in ein Sportzentrum. Sie lesen die Preisliste und vergleichen die verschiedenen Sportarten miteinander. Schreibe die Sätze ihres Gesprächs auf.

price list	price for one lesson	number of lessons
tennis	£15	15 lessons
badminton	£11	12 lessons
squash	£12	10 lessons
table tennis	£10	8 lessons

1. Ben: tennis (difficult) squash _"Tennis is more difficult than squash."_

2. Sarah: tennis (expensive) _"Tennis is the most expensive sport here."_

3. Sarah: table tennis (cheap) badminton _____

   _____

4. Ben: squash (expensive) badminton _____

   _____

5. Ben: table tennis (cheap) _____ _sport here."_

6. Sarah: squash (expensive) tennis _____

   _____

| 4 |

9

Adverbien

> **Adjektive** (*adjectives*) beschreiben **Personen und Sachen**, z. B.:
> *Here you see a **careful** driver with a **fantastic** car.*
> **Adverbien** (*adverbs*) beschreiben **Tätigkeiten**, z. B.:
> *She drives **fantastically** but **carefully**.*
>   verb   adverb   adverb
>
> Die meisten Adverbien bildet man durch das **Anhängen von -ly** an ein Adjektiv, z. B.: *a slow dance – they dance slow**ly**; a noisy city – the bus drives noisi**ly**; an angry person – he shouts angri**ly**.*
> Aber es gibt auch **unregelmäßige Adverbien**, die du lernen musst, z. B.: *fast* und *well: a fast race – he drives **fast**; a good driver – he drives **well**.*

1 Lies, wie Danas große Schwester mit ihrem neuen Motorrad fährt. An zehn Stellen im Text stehen ein Adjektiv und ein Adverb nebeneinander. Streiche an jeder Stelle das falsche Wort durch. Die Buchstaben in Klammern ergeben ein Lösungswort. Schreibe sie der Reihe nach auf die Linien.

Dana's big sister Victoria has got a new motorbike.

It's a Sunday afternoon in winter.

The road conditions* are not very good.

First Victoria rides through a little village. Here she goes slow (A) / slowly (M).

When she goes uphill, her motorbike is very noisy (O) / noisily (B). But then

it goes downhill and Victoria can go very fast. There is a forest with a lot of

high trees. She can't see very good (E) / well (T). So she must drive very

careful (H) / carefully (O). She wants to turn left after a supermarket. She

drives around the corner too quick (O) / quickly (R). There are some cows

in the field. There is a dangerous (B) / dangerously (C) level crossing.

There is a sign on the road, but she can't read it easy (K) / easily (I) because

1 Wortarten: Adjektiv und Adverb

it's a bit foggy now. Victoria tries to brake. But her brakes are very bad (K) / badly (T). A policeman stops her and asks her a lot of questions. Victoria answers them nervous (P) / nervously (E). When she stops in front of a red traffic light she is very unhappy (S) / unhappily (G).

* road conditions = Straßenverhältnisse

Victoria is interested in ___ ___ ___ ___ ___ ___ ___ ___ ___ ___ .

| 10 |

2 Übersetze bei den folgenden Sätzen das Wort in Klammern ins Englische. Trage es dann in der richtigen Form ein – als Adjektiv oder als Adverb.

1. Peter sings _____ . (gut)
2. Mr Hammond is a _____ teacher. (gut)
3. Josie is a _____ piano player. (wunderbar)
4. She plays _____ . (wunderbar)
5. This is a very _____ cow. (hungrig)
6. Josh eats his dinner _____ . (hungrig)
7. Mrs Turner is a _____ lady. (schön)
8. She plays the violin _____ . (schön)
9. We have some very _____ neighbours. (leise)
10. They always close the door very _____ . (leise)
11. Mr Brown is a _____ chess player. (schnell)
12. He wins the game very _____ . (schnell)

| 12 |

Mengenangaben: some und any

> Wenn wir von unbestimmten Mengen reden, wird **in bejahten Aussagesätzen** *some* benutzt, z. B.: *We have **some** apples.*
> **In verneinten Aussagen und Fragen** wird *any* benutzt, z. B.:
> *Do we have **any** apples? No, we don't have **any**.*

1 **Trage in die Lücken entweder *some* oder *any* ein.**

Mr Brown and Sarah have to do the shopping today.
They talk about what to buy.

Mr Brown: "Have we got _____ cornflakes left?"

Sarah: "No, we haven't got _____ . We have to buy _____."

Mr Brown: "What about coffee?"

Sarah: "That's OK. We don't need _____ .

We've still got _____ ."

Mr Brown: "I don't think we've got _____ biscuits left.

I couldn't find _____ yesterday."

Sarah: "Wait a minute. There are _____ under the coffee."

Mr Brown: "Do we need _____ jam?"

Sarah: "Yes, we need _____ . There isn't _____ left."

Mr Brown: "Fine. Let's get _____ strawberry jam this week.

And I think we need _____ bread."

Sarah: "Yes, there isn't _____ . You ate the last piece this morning."

14

12

2 Wortarten: Pronomen und Mengenangaben

★ **2** **Ergänze das Gespräch zwischen Mrs Martin und Jamie. Benutze die Angaben in Klammern und *some* oder *any*.**

Jamie doesn't like supermarkets so he always goes to Mrs Martin's shop. But Mrs Martin doesn't always have everything he needs.

Yes, I've got …	No, I haven't got …
cornflakes, coffee, strawberry jam, bread	tomatoes, French cheese, peanut butter

Jamie: "Hi Mrs Martin."
Mrs Martin: "Hello Jamie. What can I do for you?"

1. Jamie: "We need _____ cornflakes. Have you got _____?"

2. Mrs Martin: "Yes, I've got _____. Here they are."

3. Jamie: (French cheese) "OK. Have you got _____?"

4. Mrs Martin: "I'm sorry. / _____."

5. Jamie: (coffee, peanut butter) *Have* _____
   _____?"

6. Mrs Martin: _____
   _____

7. Jamie: (strawberry jam, bread): _____
   _____

8. Mrs Martin: _____.

9. Jamie: "I forgot my money! I haven't got _____ money at all! I'll run home and get _____! Sorry, Mrs Martin!"

11

13

  25 – 20 Punkte  19 – 14 Punkte  13 – 0 Punkte  Gesamtpunktzahl

Zusammensetzungen mit some / any

Die wichtigsten Zusammensetzungen (*compounds*) von *some* und *any* sind für Personen *someone* und *anyone*, für Gegenstände *something* und *anything*, für Orte *somewhere* und *anywhere*. Für sie gelten dieselben Regeln wie für *some* und *any*: **Someone, something** und **somewhere** werden **in bejahten Aussagesätzen** benutzt. **Anyone, anything** und **anywhere** benutzt man **in verneinten Aussagesätzen und in Fragen**.

1 Schreibe die folgenden Wörter in die Lücken. Streiche die Wörter durch, die du schon verwendet hast.

anyone   someone   something   anything   something   anything
somewhere   anything   someone   someone   anything

Hannah's dog Maxi ran away. Now Maxi is back home.
Mrs Pott is very angry with Maxi.

Mrs Pott: "Maxi, you stupid dog! You don't understand _____ ,

do you? When _____ calls you, you don't come.

When _____ wants to play with you, you walk away. And

now all this dirt! Is there _____ still clean in this room?

I think you spent the afternoon _____ in the forest.

Did you find _____ interesting? I'm sure you found

_____ interesting. But I don't want to know. The best

thing is I don't know _____ . One day _____

will happen to you, Maxi. I hope _____ will be there to

help you. What will happen when there isn't _____ to help

you, Maxi?"

2 Wortarten: Pronomen und Mengenangaben

2 Lies den folgenden Text und trage *some*, *any* oder ein *compound* ein.
Du musst alle angegebenen Wörter verwenden.

something   some   something   somebody   anything   anybody
anywhere   anything   anything   something   any

Doctor: "Good morning. What's the matter? How can I help you?"

Allen: "There's _____ wrong with my arm."

Doctor: "Did _____ happen to you?"

Allen: "Yes, I fell over _____ ."

Doctor: "And why?"

Allen: "Because I can't find my glasses _____ . And without my glasses I can't see _____ ."

Doctor: "Do you have _____ to put on your arm?"

Allen: "No, I haven't got _____ to put on it. Is there _____ medicine for my arm?"

Doctor: "Yes, here's _____ cream. Put it on your arm three times a day. Is there _____ here who can take you home?"

Allen: "No, but I just have to phone home and _____ can come for me."

Präpositionen des Ortes

Look at the picture. The car park is behind the supermarket.
The bank is opposite the supermarket. There is a bench in front of the tree next to the library. The church is next to the post office.

1 **Beschreibe das Bild. Verwende die vorgegebenen Textteile und die folgenden Präpositionen. Manche Präpositionen kannst du mehrmals benutzen.**

on the right/left   behind   next to   opposite   between   in front of

3 Wortarten: Präpositionen und Zahlen

1. cinema / school

2. church / museum

3. pet shop / cinema

4. book shop / butcher's shop and post office

5. café / tables and chairs

6. library / supermarket

7. bank robber / bank

8. museum / toy shop

9. café / bank

10. book shop / toy shop

10

17

   10–8 Punkte  7–5 Punkte  4–0 Punkte  Gesamtpunktzahl

Präpositionen der Zeit

1 Sieh dir Julians und Patricks Terminkalender für Dezember an. Ergänze dann den Text mit den angegebenen Präpositionen der Zeit (*prepositions of time*). Streiche die Präpositionen durch, die du schon benutzt hast.

Julian December	**Patrick** December
Monday 21st *play football evening*	Monday 21st *6.00 p.m.: meet Mark*
Tuesday 22nd	Tuesday 22nd *morning: see Doctor Baker*
Wednesday 23rd *go swimming with Dad*	Wednesday 23rd *order a pizza*
Thursday 24th – *Christmas Eve*	Thursday 24th – *Christmas Eve* *buy flowers for Mum*
Friday 25th – *Christmas Day** *visit Grandma*	Friday 25th – *Christmas Day* *9.10 a.m.: meet Shane at the station*
Saturday 26th – *Boxing Day*** *5.00 – 7.00 p.m.: play*	Saturday 26th – *Boxing Day* *6.00 – 10.00 p.m.: have a party*
Sunday 27th *10.00 a.m.: go to the sports centre with John*	Sunday 27th *get the new cinema programme*

* *Christmas Day* = erster Weihnachtsfeiertag ** *Boxing Day* = zweiter Weihnachtsfeiertag

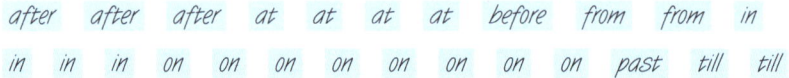

after   after   after   at   at   at   at   before   from   from   in
in   in   in   on   on   on   on   on   on   on   on   past   till   till

Julian and Patrick are talking on the phone.
Julian: "Julian Johnson speaking."
Patrick: "Hello Julian. It's me, Patrick. How are you?"
Julian: "I'm fine. And how are you?"

3 Wortarten: Präpositionen und Zahlen

Patrick: "I'm very busy _____ the moment. That's why I'm calling. We wanted to meet this week. But I think it's very difficult. Have you got your diary?"

Julian: "Yes, I've got it here."

Patrick: "What are you going to do _____ Monday?"

Julian: "_____ Monday 21st I'm going to play football _____ the evening."

Patrick: "I'm going to meet Mark _____ 6 o'clock."

Julian: "What about Tuesday morning?"

Patrick: "I'm sorry. But I've got an appointment* with Doctor Baker _____ the morning."

Julian: "_____ Wednesday, the day _____ Christmas Eve, I'm going to go swimming with Dad and then I'll be busy with my Christmas presents for Mum and Dad. The day _____ Christmas Eve, _____ Christmas Day, we are going to visit Grandma.

Patrick: "_____ ten _____ nine I'm going to meet Shane at the station _____ Christmas Day. Two days _____ Christmas Eve, _____ December 26th, we are going to have a big Christmas party _____ six _____ ten o'clock."

Julian: "_____ Boxing Day I'm going to see a play _____ five _____ seven o'clock. _____ ten o'clock _____ the morning I'm going to go to the sports centre _____ 27th December."

Patrick: "Well, let's meet _____ January _____ Christmas."

Julian: "That's a good idea. I'll call you then. Bye."

* *appointment* = Termin

25

19

   25 – 20 Punkte  19 – 13 Punkte  12 – 0 Punkte Gesamtpunktzahl

Modale Hilfsverben

> Wir benutzen ein modales Hilfsverb (*modal auxiliary*) zusammen mit einem Vollverb, um auszudrücken, was getan werden muss, kann, darf oder soll, z. B.: *You can take the book.* In der 3. Person Singular Präsens wird an modale Hilfsverben kein -s angehängt.
> Dies sind **die wichtigsten modalen Hilfsverben**:
> - **Mustn't** drückt ein **Verbot** aus, z. B.: *You mustn't eat here.* – Du darfst hier nicht essen.
> - **Needn't** drückt die **Wahlmöglichkeit** aus, z. B.: *You needn't eat this.* – Du musst das nicht essen.
> - **Must** benutzt man für „müssen" an Stelle von *have to*, um einen **Zwang** oder einen **Auftrag** auszudrücken, z. B.: *You must do this.* – Du musst das tun!

1 Shane hatte einen Unfall und muss im Bett bleiben. Trage in die Lücken ein, was er machen oder nicht machen muss, kann, soll oder darf.

can must must must mustn't mustn't mustn't needn't needn't needn't needn't needn't

1. Shane _____ get up but he _____ sleep all day.

2. He _____ watch TV but he _____ get too tired.

3. He _____ go to school for a week.

4. He _____ do any homework but he _____ learn his English vocabulary because he has a test on Monday.

5. He _____ go back to the doctor until next week but he _____ put some cream on his arm three times a day.

6. He hurt his arm and his head so he _____ move his head too much.

7. He _____ have a special diet* but he _____ drink a lot.

* *a special diet* = eine besondere Auswahl von Lebensmitteln

4 Die Zeitformen des Verbs

2 Ein Polizist redet mit einem jungen, unerfahrenen Fahrer. Schreibe *needn't*, *must* oder *mustn't* in die Lücken und vervollständige die Sätze. Unter dem Text findest du einige Vokabelhilfen.

Police officer: "Look at that sign! What does it mean?"

Learner driver: "You _____ *drive faster than* _____ ."

Police officer: "And this sign?"

Learner driver: "That means that there are traffic lights."

Police officer: "When there is a red light you _____ drive on. You _____ . You _____ stop at a zebra crossing, only when somebody wants to cross the road, then you _____ stop. You _____ switch your headlights* on in broad daylight** but you can, if you want. And this sign?"

Learner driver: "You _____ turn left. You _____ _____ ."

turn right or go straight on – rechts abbiegen oder geradeaus fahren
always stop at a red light – bleib immer an der roten Ampel stehen

* *headlights* = Scheinwerfer   ** *in broad daylight* = am helllichten Tag

simple past – Aussagesätze

Mit dem *simple past* berichtet man über Vergangenes, daher steht es oft zusammen mit Zeitangaben wie *yesterday, 15 years ago, last week*.
Das *simple past* bildet man, indem man **bei regelmäßigen Verben** (*regular verbs*) die **Endung -ed** an den Infinitiv anhängt, z. B.: *to work – he work**ed***.
Unregelmäßige Verben (*irregular verbs*) haben im *simple past* **besondere Formen**, die du auswendig lernen musst, z. B.: *to eat – she ate, to come – he came, to buy – she bought*.

1 Die Textteile in den Geschenken beschreiben, was an Hannahs Geburtstag los war. Bringe die Ereignisse in die richtige Reihenfolge. Schreibe dazu Zahlen von 1 bis 5 in die Geschenkanhänger.

Then Hannah's mother turns on the light again. The children can't see Patrick. Where is he? Then Hannah sees Patrick under the table with Maxi, her dog.

They play games. In one game Patrick turns off the light and tries to catch the other children. Suddenly he falls over something. He lies on the floor. He can't get up.

Today is Hannah's birthday. In the afternoon ten boys and girls come to her house. They all have presents for her. She takes the presents, opens them and says thank you.

At eight o'clock the party is over. The children go home and Hannah goes to her room.

Patrick has something in his hand. It's a piece of cake. But Maxi likes the birthday cake, too and eats it with a smile on his face.

5

4 Die Zeitformen des Verbs

2 Nach der Party schreibt Hannah in ihr Tagebuch. Vervollständige ihre Eintragung. Benutze dazu die Textteile aus Aufgabe 1. Schreibe in der Ich-Form und im *simple past*.

Friday, 22nd April

Dear Diary*,

Today was my birthday. In the afternoon, ten boys and girls came to my house.

They all _____

* *diary* = Tagebuch

simple past – Fragesätze

> Fragen mit *Who* und *What* können nach einem Subjekt oder einem Objekt fragen. Wenn nach dem **Objekt** gefragt wird, muss in der Frage *do* bzw. *does* (*simple present*) oder *did* (*simple past*) benutzt werden, z. B.: *Who did Patrick write to?* – An wen schrieb Patrick?
> Wenn nach dem **Subjekt** gefragt wird, wird kein *do*, *does* oder *did* in der Frage benutzt, z. B.: *Who wrote to Patrick?* – Wer schrieb Patrick?

1 **Patrick hat seinem Freund Julian eine E-Mail geschrieben. Er beantwortet darin zehn Fragen, die Julian ihm zuvor gestellt hatte.**
Lies die E-Mail und schreibe die übrigen neun Fragen im *simple past* auf.
Tipp: Nach den unterstrichenen Angaben fragst du mit den folgenden Fragewörtern: *how, how long, what, when, where*.

London, 25th August
Dear Julian,

Thank you for your email. Now I can answer all your questions. I went to Spain on holiday this summer. No, I didn't go alone, I went with my parents. We stayed there for two weeks. The weather was sunny and warm. Yes, I went swimming every day. No, the water wasn't very cold. Yes, I met a lot of girls. I played volleyball with them. No, I didn't see any sharks*, because there are no sharks in Spain.
I got back to London on 20th August.

Love, Patrick

* *shark* = Haifisch

4 Die Zeitformen des Verbs

1. *Where did you go on holiday this summer?*
2. _____
3. _____
4. _____
5. _____
6. _____
7. _____
8. _____
9. _____
10. _____ ⟨9⟩

★ **2** Schreibe zu den folgenden Sätzen jeweils eine Frage nach dem Subjekt und eine Frage nach dem Objekt im *simple past*.

1. The animals ate the fruits. *Who ate the fruits? What did the animals eat?*
2. My father cleaned the table. _____
3. The children helped Mr Pott. _____
4. Sarah caught the ball. _____

pro richtige Frage 1 Punkt ⟨6⟩

25

  15–12 Punkte  11–8 Punkte  7–0 Punkte Gesamtpunktzahl

simple past – Aussagen, Verneinungen, Fragen

1 Lies die beiden Postkarten. Schreibe dann mit den angegebenen Satzteilen Aussagesätze (✓), Negativsätze (✗) oder Fragen (?) im *simple past* auf. Schreibe bei Fragesätzen auch die Antworten dazu.

Dear Mum,

We are having a lovely time here in Portsmouth. The weather is great and the hotel is OK. But the food isn't very good. We went swimming before breakfast. Last night Susan and I went to a disco. It was great. I met a nice boy!

Love,
Sarah

Mrs Brown

22 Green Road

Sheffield XCF 123

England

Dear Bernhard,

It's great here in France. It's hot and the water's warm. I spoke French to the waiters in the hotel yesterday. And I watched French TV in the evening.

Yours,
Peter

Bernhard Dobbs

8 London Road

Edinburgh BYS 129

Scotland

1. where / Sarah / to go on holiday (?) *Where did Sarah go on holiday?*

   She went to Portsmouth on holiday.

4 Die Zeitformen des Verbs

2. where / Sarah / to stay (?) _____

3. Sarah / to go for a swim / before dinner (✘) _____

4. Sarah / to go / disco / last night (✔) _____

5. who / to go / Portsmouth / with Sarah (?) _____

6. Sarah / to meet / boy / disco (✔) _____

7. where / Peter / to go on holiday (?) _____

8. Peter / to have / good weather (✔) _____

9. who / Peter / to speak to / yesterday (?) _____

10. Peter / to watch / French TV / all day (✘) _____

11. Peter / to write to / postcard / his mother (✘) _____

14

27

Vermischte Übungen

Hier kannst du überprüfen, was du schon kannst.
Tipp: Wenn du Schwierigkeiten hast, schau auf den in Klammern angegebenen Seiten nach.

1 Übersetze die folgenden Sätze. (Seite 4–9)

1. Ein Motorrad ist gefährlicher als ein Auto.

   _____

2. Ein Lkw ist schwerer als ein Motorrad.

   _____

3. Ein Motorrad ist schneller als ein Auto.

   _____

4. Ein Sportwagen ist interessanter als ein Lkw.

   _____

pro richtigen Satz 2 Punkte   8

2 In den folgenden Sätzen ist entweder das Adjektiv oder das Adverb richtig. Streiche die falsche Form durch. (Seite 10–11)

1. My father always drives very careful / carefully.
2. Tom spoke very slow / slowly.
3. A very angry / angrily police officer talked to Victoria.
4. Lisa plays chess good / well.
5. She's a good / well player.
6. Mrs Pott smiles happy / happily.
7. Hannah's dog Maxi sits under the table quietly / quiet.
8. Peter told his father a funny / funnily joke.

8

Lösungen

★ Aufgaben mit höherem Schwierigkeitsgrad

1 Wortarten: Adjektiv und Adverb

Seite 4–5

1
2. The town is cleaner than the city.
3. The village is smaller than the town.
4. The city is bigger than the town.
5. The town is dirtier than the village.
6. The town is smaller than the city.
7. The village is quieter than the town.
8. The town is bigger than the village.
9. The city is noisier than the town.
10. The town is quieter than the city.
11. The city is busier than the town.

2
1. better
2. worse
3. biggest
4. smallest

Seite 6–7

1
2. The truck is more powerful than the van. / The van is less powerful than the truck.
3. The van is more powerful than the family car. / The family car is less powerful than the van.
4. The family car is more useful than the sports car. / The sports car is less useful than the family car.
5. The sports car is more expensive than the van. / The van is less expensive than the sports car.
6. The truck is the most expensive car.

2 ★
2. The family car is more comfortable than the sports car. / The sports car is less comfortable than the family car.
3. The family car is more useful than the sports car for a family. / The sports car is less useful than a family car for a family.
4. The sports car is the most beautiful car.
5. The family car is the best for me.

Seite 8–9

1/**2**

Adjektiv	Komparativ	Superlativ
nice	nicer	nicest
wide	wider	widest
fine	finer	finest
short	shorter	shortest
loud	louder	loudest
old	older	oldest
big	bigger	biggest
hot	hotter	hottest
red	redder	reddest
easy	easier	easiest
heavy	heavier	heaviest
silly	sillier	silliest
famous	more famous	most famous
nervous	more nervous	most nervous
useful	more useful	most useful
dangerous	more dangerous	most dangerous
intelligent	more intelligent	most intelligent
beautiful	more beautiful	most beautiful

3
3. "Table tennis is cheaper than badminton."
4. "Squash is more expensive than badminton."
5. "Table tennis is the cheapest sport here."
6. "Squash is less expensive than tennis."

Seite 10–11

1 Richtig sind:
slowly, noisy, well, carefully, quickly, dangerous, easily, bad, nervously, unhappy

Victoria is interested in motorbikes.

2 1. well, 2. good, 3. wonderful, 4. wonderfully, 5. hungry, 6. hungrily, 7. beautiful, 8. beautifully, 9. quiet, 10. quietly, 11. quick, 12. quickly

Lösungen

2 Wortarten: Pronomen und Mengenangaben

Seite 12–13

① any, any, some, any, some,
any, any, some, any, some,
any, some, some, any

② ★ 1. some, any
2. some
3. "Have you got any French cheese?"
4. "I haven't (have not) got any French cheese."
5. "Have you got any coffee and any peanut butter?"
6. "I've (I have) got some coffee but I haven't (have not) got any peanut butter."
7. "Have you got any strawberry jam and any bread?"
8. "Yes, I've (I have) got some strawberry jam and some bread."
9. "I haven't got any money at all! I'll run home and get some!"

Seite 14–15

① anything, someone, someone,
anything, somewhere, anything,
something, anything,
something, someone, anyone

② something, something, something,
anywhere, anything, anything, anything,
any, some, anybody, somebody

3 Wortarten: Präpositionen und Zahlen

Seite 16–17

① 1. The cinema is next to the school (on the right).
2. The church is opposite the museum.
3. The pet shop is opposite the cinema.
4. The book shop is between the butcher's shop and the post office.
5. In front of the café there are tables and chairs. Oder: There are tables and chairs in front of the café.
6. The library is behind (next to / in front of) the supermarket.
7. The bank robber is in front of the bank.
8. The museum is next to the toy shop (on the left).
9. The café is behind (next to) the bank.
10. The book shop is opposite the toy shop.

Seite 18–19

① at, on, On, in, at, in,
On, before, after, on, At,
past, on, after, on,
from, till, On, from, till,
At, in, on, in, after

4 Die Zeitformen des Verbs

Seite 20 – 21

1
1. mustn't (needn't)
   needn't (mustn't)
2. can
   mustn't
3. needn't
4. needn't
   must
5. needn't
   must
6. mustn't
7. needn't
   must

2
mustn't
50 mph
mustn't
must always stop at a red light
needn't
must
needn't
mustn't
must turn right or go straight on

Seite 22 – 23

1
1. Today is Hannah's birthday ...
2. They play games ...
3. Then Hannah's mother ...
4. Patrick has something ...
5. At eight o'clock ...

2 They all <u>had</u> presents for <u>me</u>. <u>I</u> <u>took</u> the presents, <u>opened</u> them and <u>said</u> thank you. <u>We</u> <u>played</u> games. In one game Patrick <u>turned</u> off the light and <u>tried</u> to catch the other children. Suddenly he <u>fell</u> over something. He <u>lay</u> on the floor. He <u>couldn't</u> get up. <u>My</u> mother <u>turned</u> on the light again. <u>We</u> <u>couldn't</u> see Patrick. Where <u>was</u> he? Then <u>I</u> <u>saw</u> Patrick under the table with Maxi, <u>my</u> dog. Patrick <u>had</u> something in his hand. It <u>was</u> a piece of cake. But Maxi <u>liked</u> the birthday cake, too and <u>ate</u> it with a smile on his face. At eight o'clock the party <u>was</u> over. The children <u>went</u> home and <u>I</u> <u>went</u> to <u>my</u> room.

Seite 24 – 25

1
2. Did you go alone?
3. How long did you stay?
4. How was the weather?
5. Did you go swimming every day?
6. Was the water very cold?
7. Did you meet a lot of girls?
8. What did you play with them?
9. Did you see any sharks?
10. When did you get back to London?

2 ★
2. Who cleaned the table?
   What did my father clean?
3. Who helped Mr Pott?
   Who did the children help?
4. Who caught the ball?
   What did Sarah catch?

Seite 26 – 27

1
2. Where did Sarah stay?
   She stayed in a hotel in Portsmouth.
3. Sarah didn't go for a swim before dinner.
4. Sarah went to a disco last night.
5. Who went to Portsmouth with Sarah?
   Susan went to Portsmouth with Sarah.
6. Sarah met a boy at the disco.
7. Where did Peter go on holiday?
   Peter went to France.
8. Peter had good weather.
9. Who did Peter speak to yesterday?
   Peter spoke to the waiters in the hotel yesterday.
10. Peter didn't watch French TV all day.
11. Peter didn't write a postcard to his mother.

Lösungen

Seite 28 / 37

❶
1. A motorbike is more dangerous than a car.
2. A truck is heavier than a motorbike.
3. A motorbike is faster than a car.
4. A sports car is more interesting than a truck.

❷ Richtig sind:
1. carefully
2. slowly
3. angry
4. well
5. good
6. happily
7. quietly
8. funny

❸ in, at, in, in

❹ 1. any, 2. some, 3. any, 4. anything, 5. something

❺ Last Monday the weather <u>was</u> fine and Hannah <u>went</u> to town. She <u>didn't</u> go by bus, she <u>went</u> by bike. Hannah <u>took</u> her dog Maxi with her. Maxi <u>ran</u> very fast. When Hannah <u>came</u> home, she <u>played</u> basketball with her friends. In the evening she <u>read</u> a book.

Seite 38 – 39

❶
2. The referee acts fairly these days, too.
3. There are sponsors for each team these days, too.
4. The fans come to the game every week these days, too.
5. Fair play is very important these days, too.
6. The players run very fast these days, too.
7. The players like their fans these days, too.

❷ ★
2. Yes, when I was young you could buy tea in the stadium, too.
3. No, when I was young there weren't (were not) any hooligans.
4. No, when I was young the players paid for their football boots.
5. Yes, when I was young lots of fans watched the game on television, too.
6. Yes, when I was young each team had its own doctor, too.
7. No, when I was young the players didn't (did not) get a lot of money.
8. Yes, when I was young a lot of good players went to Italian football clubs, too.

Seite 40 – 41

❶
did
Did
didn't
do
do
Do
do
don't
Do
do
Does
doesn't
Do
do
Does
does
doesn't
Did
didn't
Do
don't
do
Do
Did
didn't
Does
does

Seite 42 – 43

1
2. I think I will do more sports next year.
3. I hope I will get my own TV next year.
4. I think it will rain very often next year.
5. I hope we will go on holiday to the sea next year.
6. I hope I will celebrate my 70th birthday with the family next year.

2
1. I promise I will take the dog for a walk more often next year.
2. I promise I will go shopping once a week next year.
3. I promise I will stop smoking cigars in the living room next year.

Seite 44 – 45

1
Well, in London it's <u>going to be</u> very overcast with heavy rain.
In Scotland <u>it is going to be</u> sunny and a bit cloudy.
In the east of England <u>it's going to be</u> rainy.
In Northern Ireland <u>it is going to be</u> cloudy and rainy with some sunny spells.
<u>I'm (I am) going to climb</u> Mount Snowdon tomorrow. Now tell me what the weather <u>is going to be</u> like for Mount Snowdon tomorrow.
No, <u>it isn't (is not) going to rain</u>. There is <u>going to be</u> glorious sunshine.

Seite 46 – 47

1
1. will be
2. will win
3. is going to watch
4. isn't (is not) going to watch
5. will probably tell
6. will understand
7. will tell
8. will be, is going to try
9. will watch
10. are going to go

2 ★ 2. Will Hannah go to the cinema with Ben?
3. What is Jamie going to do after school?
4. Is Mr Pott going to watch the tennis match this evening?
5. Will Sarah do her homework tomorrow?
6. Where will Mr and Mrs Brown stay in their holidays?
7. Are Ben and Jamie going to play football next week?
8. Will Josh tell his best friend a secret?

Seite 48 – 49

1
2. Josh has already put the dishes on the shelf.
3. Hannah has just put the milk into the fridge.
4. They have just cleaned the floor.
5. Josh has already taken out the rubbish.
6. Josh and Hannah have just made a cake.
7. Hannah has just watered the plants.
8. They have already gone shopping.
9. Josh has just fed Maxi.

Lösungen

Seite 50–51

❶
2. I haven't learned (learnt) <u>any</u> history yet.
3. I haven't finished the picture yet.
4. I haven't bought a new exercise book yet.
5. I haven't drawn a map of Great Britain yet.
6. I haven't collected <u>any</u> flowers yet.
7. I haven't learned (learnt) my English vocabulary yet.
8. I haven't repaired my school bag yet.
9. I haven't written a story yet.
10. I haven't written a German essay yet.
11. I haven't made a survey about the traffic in our town yet.
12. I haven't read the end of the book about Robin Hood yet.

❷
1. She hasn't done her maths homework yet.
5. She hasn't drawn a map of Great Britain yet.
6. She hasn't collected <u>any</u> flowers yet.
9. She hasn't written a story yet.

Seite 52–53

❶
1. <u>Have</u> you ever <u>had</u> a pet?
2. <u>Have</u> you always <u>kept</u> your dogs in the house?
3. <u>Have</u> you always <u>given</u> your dog proper food?
4. Why <u>have</u> you <u>decided</u> to buy another dog?
5. Why <u>have</u> you <u>come</u> to the animal shelter?

❷
2. "Where have you put the brown rabbit?"
"I've (I have) put the brown rabbit in the birdcage."
3. "What has happened to the parrot?"
"Nothing has happened to the parrot."
4. "Have you fed the cats in room six?"
"I've (I have) fed the cats in room four."
5. "Have you taken the dogs for a walk?"
"I've (I have) played with the dogs."

Seite 54–55

❶
booked
picked up
haven't (have not) got
Have you decided
talked
Did you phone
called
hasn't (has not) come
checked
has come
has just brought
haven't (have not) asked
checked
were
haven't (have not) looked

❷ ★
1. I met Peter two years ago.
2. He has been a good friend ever since.
3. I met him last Saturday.
4. He hasn't (has not) phoned me yet.

Seite 56–57

1
1. will I get
2. will get
3. needed
   bought
4. wanted
   gave
5. tell
   forgets
6. isn't (is not)
7. don't (do not) want
   don't (do not) like
8. need
9. buys
10. will get
11. will buy
12. will get
13. will buy

2
1. help
2. need
   haven't (have not) decided
3. do you take
4. take
5. Have you ever had
6. haven't (have not)
7. got
   are
   will go
8. don't (do not) like
   bought
9. am
   haven't (have not) got
   will get
10. will come

Seite 58–59

1 went, was, crossed, crashed, broke, sprained, had, took, x-rayed, did, read, played, got, liked, was, loved, was, was, had, were, couldn't

2 ★
2. "Did you ride very fast on your mountain bike?"
3. "Did the boy on the skateboard cross the street?"
4. "Have you been in the same class for a long time?"
5. "Are you friends?"
6. "Where did the ambulance take you?"
7. "What did the doctor do?"
8. "When did you have your first accident?"
9. "What about Chris? Has he ever had an accident before?"
10. "Will you go to school tomorrow?"

5 Der Satz

Seite 60–61

①
2. You should send your letters at the beginning of December.
3. You should write the address on the front of the envelope.
4. Don't forget to put the stamp in the right corner.
5. Do you want to send it by airmail?
6. Then put an airmail sticker on the envelope.
7. Do not forget to put the letter into the postbox.

②
2. "I need ten stamps for postcards to Germany."
3. "And I need one stamp for a postcard to the USA."
4. "Yes, I'd like to send it by airmail."
5. "Have you got any nice stamps?"
6. "Can you put on the airmail sticker for me, please?"
7. "Thank you very much."

Seite 62–63

①
1. Where does Mr Brown work on Saturday afternoons?
2. What did she buy?
3. When do the Millers always get up?
4. Where do the children never play football?

②
1. will be
2. is going to start
3. are going to play
4. is going to rain

③ Richtig sind:
1. will rain
2. bought
3. haven't done

④
1. Peter has just done his homework.
2. Have the boys gone shopping yet?
3. John hasn't (has not) bought a new exercise book yet.

⑤ ★ saw
haven't (have not) seen
asked
didn't (did not) know
called
came
have you seen
asked
said
stole

4 Die Zeitformen des Verbs

3 Schreibe die richtigen Präpositionen in die Lücken. (Seite 18–19)

We can meet _____ two hours. I'm very busy _____ the moment.

Tom's birthday is _____ July. Which year was he born _____ ?

| 4 |

4 Schreibe *some*, *any*, *something* oder *anything* in die Lücken. (Seite 12–15)

1. Have you got _____ apples?
2. I need _____ apples.
3. I'm sorry, but I haven't got _____ apples today.
4. Is there _____ else I can do for you?
5. Yesterday I bought _____ nice for your birthday.

| 5 |

5 Unterstreiche im folgenden Text die Verben und schreibe den Text dann im *simple past* auf. (Seite 22–23)

Every Monday when the weather is fine Hannah goes to town. She doesn't go by bus, she goes by bike. Hannah takes her dog Maxi with her. Maxi runs very fast. When Hannah comes home, she plays basketball with her friends. In the evening she reads a book.

Last Monday the weather was fine and _____

_____

_____

_____

_____

pro richtiges Verb 1 Punkt | 8 |

37

  33–27 Punkte  26–18 Punkte  17–0 Punkte   Gesamt-punktzahl

simple present und simple past (1)

1 Grandpa Brown erinnert sich an den Fußball zu seiner Jugendzeit. Sein Enkel Ben bestätigt, dass es heute genauso ist. Schreibe auf, was Ben sagt. Benutze das *simple present*.

1. Mr Brown: "When I was young the players practised four times a week."

   Ben: "*They practise four times a week these days*, too.*"

2. Mr Brown: "When I was young the referee** acted fairly."

   Ben: "_____ these days, too."

3. Mr Brown: "When I was young there were sponsors for each team."

   Ben: "_____ these days, too."

4. Mr Brown: "When I was young the fans came to the game every week."

   Ben: "_____ these days, too."

5. Mr Brown: "When I was young fair play was very important."

   Ben: "_____ these days, too."

6. Mr Brown: "When I was young the players ran really fast."

   Ben: "_____ these days, too."

7. Mr Brown: "When I was young the players liked their fans."

   Ben: "_____ these days, too."

* *these days* = heutzutage
** *referee* = Schiedsrichter

| 6 |

★ **2** Ben erzählt, was heute so alles beim Fußball passiert. Grandpa Brown sagt, dass es früher manchmal anders und manchmal genauso war. Schreibe auf, was Grandpa Brown sagt. Benutze das *simple past*.

1. Ben: "Today lots of fans buy season tickets."

4 Die Zeitformen des Verbs

Mr Brown: *"Oh no: When I was young the fans didn't buy season tickets."*

2. Ben: "Today you can buy tea in the stadium."

   Mr Brown: "Yes, when I was young _____

   _____, too."

3. Ben: "Today there are lots of hooligans."

   Mr Brown: "No, when I was young _____ any _____."

4. Ben: "Today the players don't pay for their football boots."

   Mr Brown: "Oh, really?! No, when I was young _____

   _____."

5. Ben: "Today lots of fans watch the game on television."

   Mr Brown: "Yes, when I was young _____

   _____, too."

6. Ben: "Today each team has its own doctor."

   Mr Brown: "Yes, when I was young _____

   _____, too."

7. Ben: "Today the players get a lot of money."

   Mr Brown: "No, when I was young _____."

8. Ben: "Today a lot of good players go to Italian football clubs."

   Mr Brown: "Yes, when I was young _____

   _____, too."   7

simple present und simple past (2)

1 Ergänze den Text mit den angegebenen Formen von *to do*. Streiche die Formen durch, die du schon benutzt hast. Eine Form bleibt übrig.

> does   didn't   do   did   do   doesn't   do   didn't   do   does   did
> do   do   doesn't   did   do   does   do   don't   do   does   do
> does   did   do   don't   didn't

This is an interview with the famous basketball player Michelle Towers.

Interviewer: "Hello, Ms Towers. I'd like to ask you some questions. When _____ you start playing basketball?"

Michelle: "I started playing basketball fifteen years ago."

Interviewer: "_____ you join a basketball club when you were six?"

Michelle: "No, I _____. I played in the streets."

Interviewer: "How often _____ you play basketball now?"

Michelle: "Normally I play five times a week."

Interviewer: "How many hours _____ you play every day?"

Michelle: "Sometimes I play for four hours, sometimes for five or six."

Interviewer: "_____ you have time for other things?"

Michelle: "Oh yes, I _____. When I _____ play basketball, I listen to music, go shopping or work in my garden."

Interviewer: "_____ you have any brothers or sisters?"

Michelle: "Yes, I _____. I have one brother."

Interviewer: "_____ he play basketball, too?"

4 Die Zeitformen des Verbs

Michelle: "No, he _____. He hates it."

Interviewer: "_____ your parents like basketball?"

Michelle: "Yes, they _____."

Interviewer: "_____ your father read a lot about basketball?"

Michelle: "Yes, he _____. He reads a lot, but he _____ watch basketball games on TV."

Interviewer: "_____ your father play basketball when he was young?"

Michelle: "No, he _____. He wasn't tall enough."

Interviewer: "_____ you eat anything special before a basketball game?"

Michelle: "No, I _____. I eat whatever I like."

Interviewer: "When _____ you go to bed?"

Michelle: "I go to bed at nine o'clock."

Interviewer: "_____ the games start in the morning?"

Michelle: "No, they normally start in the afternoon."

Interviewer: "_____ your parents watch every game you played in last year?"

Michelle: "No, they _____."

Interviewer: "_____ your mother like basketball, too?"

Michelle: "Yes, she _____."

Interviewer: "Thank your for the interview, Ms Towers."

27

41

  27–23 Punkte  22–15 Punkte  14–0 Punkte Gesamtpunktzahl

will-future

Das **Futur mit will (will-future)** beschreibt **unveränderbare zukünftige Ereignisse** und drückt **Hoffnungen** für oder **Vermutungen** über die Zukunft aus. Es wird gebildet aus *will* und dem Infinitiv eines Verbs. Die Kurzform von *will* ist *'ll*.
Das *will-future* hat für alle Personen die gleiche Form, z. B.:
We **will** (oder: We**'ll**) *leave together.* You **will** (oder: You**'ll**) *leave tomorrow.*
He **will** (oder: He**'ll**) *leave tomorrow.* I **will** (oder: I**'ll**) *leave tomorrow.*
Sehr oft steht das *will-future* nach diesen Verben: *to think, to hope, to expect, to promise.*

1 Die Mitglieder der Familie Brown denken über das nächste Jahr nach. Sie haben sehr unterschiedliche Erwartungen, Hoffnungen und auch Befürchtungen. Sieh dir die Bilder an. Bilde dann aus den angegebenen Satzteilen Sätze mit dem *will-future*.

1. Mr Brown: I / to buy / a new car / next year

   I think I will buy a new car next year.

4 Die Zeitformen des Verbs

2. Mrs Brown: I / to do / more sports / next year

   I think _____ .

3. Sarah: I / to get / my own TV / next year

   I hope _____ .

4. Jamie: to rain / very often / next year

   I think _____ .

5. Ben: we / to go on holiday / to the sea / next year

   I hope _____ .

6. Grandpa Brown: to celebrate / 70th birthday / with the family / next year

   I hope _____ .

   pro richtige Zeit 1 Punkt; pro richtige Wortstellung 1 Punkt [10]

2 Einige Familienmitglieder haben gute Vorsätze für das nächste Jahr gefasst. Bilde Sätze mit dem *will-future*.

1. Sarah: to take / the dog / for a walk / more often / next year

   I promise I will _____ .

2. Mr Brown: to go shopping / once a week / next year

   I promise _____ .

3. Grandpa Brown: to stop / smoking cigars / in the living room / next year

   I promise _____ .

   pro richtige Zeit 1 Punkt; pro richtige Wortstellung 1 Punkt [6]

  16 – 14 Punkte  13 – 9 Punkte  8 – 0 Punkte  Gesamt-punktzahl

going to-future

> Das **Futur mit *going to*** (***going to-future***) drückt ein **unmittelbar bevorstehendes Ereignis**, ein **Vorhaben**, einen **Plan** oder eine **Absicht** aus.
> Das Futur mit *going to* besteht aus drei Teilen: aus *am/is/are*, *going to* und dem Infinitiv des Verbs, z. B.: *I **am going to do** my homework.*
> *He **is going to climb** the mountain.*

London: *very overcast with heavy rain* = stark bewölkt mit strömendem Regen
Wales: *glorious sunshine* = strahlender Sonnenschein
Scotland: *sunny and a bit cloudy* = sonnig und leicht bewölkt
Northern Ireland: *cloudy, rainy with some sunny spells* = bewölkt, Regen mit sonnigen Abschnitten
the east of England: *rainy*

1 Ergänze mithilfe der Textteile unter dem Bild die Lücken in dem Gespräch zwischen Josh und Ben. Schreibe im *going to-future*.

Josh and his parents are in Wales, at the foot of Snowdon*. Josh wants to climb Snowdon tomorrow. He phones his cousin Ben to find out what the weather will be like.

Josh: "Hi, Ben. Did you see the weather forecast on TV? I want to know what the weather *is going to be* like on Mount Snowdon."

4 Die Zeitformen des Verbs

Ben: "Hi, Josh. Well, in London it's _____

_____."

Josh: "I don't want to know about London. Is it going to rain in Wales?"

Ben: "Wait a minute. In Scotland it _____

_____."

Josh: "Not Scotland: What about Mount Snowdon?"

Ben: "In the east of England it's _____."

Josh: "No, not England. Listen: I am in North Wales!"

Ben: "Oh, oh. In Northern Ireland it _____

_____."

Josh: "Ben! What about Mount Snowdon?"

Ben: "Why do you want to know? What are you going to do there?"

Josh: "I _____ Mount Snowdon tomorrow. Now tell me what the weather _____ like for Mount Snowdon tomorrow."

Ben: "Have you got a good anorak with you?"

Josh: "Yes, is it going to rain?"

Ben: "No, it _____ . There is _____ sunshine. So you can leave your anorak at your hotel!"

* Mount Snowdon is the highest mountain in Wales and England.

für jede richtige Verbform 2 Punkte   16

45

will-future und going to-future

> Das **will-future** drückt eher unsichere Vorhersagen und Vermutungen über Dinge aus, die man nicht beeinflussen kann.
> Oft steht es nach *maybe, I think, I hope, I promise*.
> Das **going to-future** bringt ein festes Vorhaben oder eine sichere Ankündigung für die Zukunft zum Ausdruck.

1 Schreibe die richtige Futurform des Verbs in Klammern in die Lücken (*will-future* oder *going to-future*).

1. I think it _____ (to be) an interesting game tonight.

2. I'm sure Schalke _____ (to win).

3. My Dad _____ (to watch) the game with me on TV.

4. My sister _____ (not to watch) the game with us. She hates football.

5. She _____ probably _____ (to tell) us again how stupid football is.

6. I hope one day she _____ (to understand) us.

7. Maybe Daddy _____ (to tell) her some interesting things about football.

8. It _____ (to be) hard, but he _____ (to try).

9. Maybe we _____ (to watch) football with the whole family one day!

10. But tonight Mum and my sister _____ (to go) to the cinema.

|11|

4 Die Zeitformen des Verbs

> **Fragen** bildet man im **will-future** mit *will* und dem Infinitiv des Verbs, z. B.:
> *Will she leave tomorrow? Will they go on holiday next week?*
> Beim **going to-future** bestehen Fragen aus einer Form von *to be*, aus *going to* und dem Infinitiv des Verbs, z. B.: *Is he going to watch TV this evening?*
> Auch kann man im *going to-* und *will-future* Fragen mit Fragewörtern bilden, z. B.: *What will he say to her? When are they going to go to Spain?*

★ **2** **Bilde mit den angegebenen Satzteilen Fragesätze im *going to-future* (g) oder im *will-future* (w).**

1. it / to be / hot / next summer (w) <u>*Will it be hot next summer?*</u>

2. Hannah / to go / cinema / with Ben (w)

   _____ ?

3. what / Jamie / to do / after school (g)

   _____ ?

4. Mr Pott / to watch / the tennis match / this evening (g)

   _____ ?

5. Sarah / to do / her homework / tomorrow (w)

   _____ ?

6. where / Mr and Mrs Brown / to stay / in their holidays (w)

   _____ ?

7. Ben and Jamie / to play / football / next week (g)

   _____ ?

8. Josh / to tell / his best friend / a secret (w)

   _____ ?   7

present perfect – Aussagesätze

Das *present perfect* wird für Handlungen benutzt,
- die **in der Vergangenheit stattgefunden** haben, aber ein **Ergebnis in der Gegenwart** haben;
- die **in der Vergangenheit begonnen** haben und **immer noch andauern**.

Das *present perfect* wird gebildet aus *have/has* und der 3. Form des Verbs (*past participle*).
Die 3. Verbform hat bei regelmäßigen Verben dieselbe Form wie das *simple past*, z. B.: *I **have** cleaned my room.*
Bei unregelmäßigen Verben musst du die 3. Verbform auswendig lernen, z. B.: *She **has** already **seen** the film.   They **have** just **gone**.*

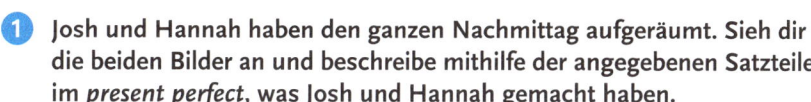

4 Die Zeitformen des Verbs

1 Josh und Hannah haben den ganzen Nachmittag aufgeräumt. Sieh dir die beiden Bilder an und beschreibe mithilfe der angegebenen Satzteile im *present perfect*, was Josh und Hannah gemacht haben.

1. Josh and Hannah / the dishes / to wash / just

   Josh and Hannah have just washed the dishes.

2. Josh / on the shelf / to put / the dishes / already

   _____

3. the milk / Hannah / to put / into the fridge / just

   _____

4. they / the floor / to clean / just

   _____

5. Josh / to take out / the rubbish / already

   _____

6. a cake / Josh and Hannah / to make / just

   _____

7. to water / the plants / Hannah / just

   _____

8. they / to go shopping / already

   _____

9. Josh / to feed / Maxi / just

   _____

pro richtige Zeit 1 Punkt; pro richtige Wortstellung 1 Punkt   16

49

present perfect – Verneinungen

> Die Verneinung des *present perfect* ist ganz einfach: Hinter *have* bzw. *has* kommt ein *not*, z. B.: He **has not** clos**ed** the window.
> Bei „noch-nicht-Sätzen" steht im Englischen meist *yet* am Ende des Satzes, z. B.: *I **haven't** seen this film **yet***. – Ich habe diesen Film noch nicht gesehen.

It's 3 o'clock on a sunny Monday afternoon.
Here's Sarah's homework list for this week:

This week's homework:

1. *do maths homework*
2. *learn some history*
3. *finish the picture*
4. *buy a new exercise book*
5. *draw a map of Great Britain*
6. *collect some flowers*
7. *learn my English vocabulary*
8. *repair my school bag*
9. *write a story*
10. *write a German essay*
11. *make a survey* about the traffic in our town*
12. *read the end of the book about Robin Hood*

* *survey* = Untersuchung, Umfrage

On her way home from school Sarah met her friend Celia. The two girls went to a cafeteria and had a lemonade.
Now it's 5 o'clock.
Look at Sarah's homework list.

4 Die Zeitformen des Verbs

1 Schreibe im *present perfect* auf, was Sarah alles noch nicht getan hat.

1. _I haven't done my maths homework yet._
2. _____
3. _____
4. _____
5. _____
6. _____
7. _____
8. _____
9. _____
10. _____
11. _____
12. _____ | 11 |

2 Schreibe zu den Sätzen 1, 5, 6 und 9, was Celia über Sarah sagt.

1. _She _____ her _____ yet._
5. _____ .
6. _____ .
9. _____ . | 4 |

51

    15–12 Punkte    11–8 Punkte    7–0 Punkte    Gesamt-punktzahl

present perfect – Fragesätze

> Um im *present perfect* eine **Frage** zu bilden, muss *have/has* vor das Subjekt an den Anfang des Satzes gestellt werden, z. B.:
> *Has she gone home already?* – Ist sie schon nach Hause gegangen?

Hannah möchte einen zweiten Hund aus dem Tierheim (*animal shelter*) holen, damit Maxi nicht so alleine ist. Mrs Fields vom Tierheim stellt ihr viele Fragen, um zu erfahren, ob Hannah etwas von Tieren versteht.

1 **Schreibe die Verben in Klammern im *present perfect* in die Lücken.**

1. Mrs Fields: "_____ you ever _____ a pet?" (to have)

   Hannah: "Yes, we have always had dogs at home."

2. Mrs Fields: "_____ you always _____ your dogs in the

   house?" (to keep) Hannah: "Yes, we have."

3. Mrs Fields: "_____ you always _____ your dog proper food?"

   (to give)

   Hannah: "Yes, we have always given our dogs good dog food."

4. Mrs Fields: "Why _____ you _____ to buy another

   dog?" (to decide)

   Hannah: "Because our dog Maxi needs a friend to play with."

5. Mrs Fields: "Why _____ you _____ to the animal shelter?"

   (to come)

   Hannah: "Because I have heard that there are many poor, homeless dogs

   here. I want to help."

pro richtiges Prädikat (2 Teile!) 2 Punkte   10

4 Die Zeitformen des Verbs

2 Weil Mrs Fields einen Arzttermin hat, muss ihr Mitarbeiter Curt sie vertreten. Mrs Fields ruft ihn später mit dem Handy an. Schreibe ihre Fragen und Curts Antworten mithilfe der Satzteile im *present perfect* auf.

1. Mrs Fields: what / to do / with the two white mice?
   "*What have you done with the two white mice?*"
   Curt: to take / them / home "*I have taken them home*".

2. Mrs Fields: where / to put / the brown rabbit?

   Curt: to put / the brown rabbit / in the birdcage

3. Mrs Fields: what / to happen / to the parrot?

   Curt: nothing / to happen / to the parrot

4. Mrs Fields: to feed / the cats in room six?

   Curt: to feed / the cats in room four

5. Mrs Fields: to take / the dogs / for a walk?

   Curt: to play / with the dogs

present perfect und simple past

> Das **present perfect** steht sehr oft in Sätzen, die die folgenden **Zeitangaben** enthalten: *already, not yet, ever, never, until now* und *just*.
> Ein Vorgang hat in der Vergangenheit begonnen, dauert aber vielleicht noch bis jetzt an oder hat jetzt ein Ergebnis.
> Das **simple past** finden wir häufig bei diesen **Zeitangaben**: *yesterday, two days/weeks/months/years ago, last Monday/year ...*
> Eine Handlung ist in der Vergangenheit zu einem bestimmten Zeitpunkt abgeschlossen worden.

1 Entscheide, ob in den folgenden Sätzen das Verb in Klammern im *present perfect* oder im *simple past* geschrieben werden muss.

Mr and Mrs Brown are talking to a bank manager.

Bank manager: "Good morning. Can I help you?"

Mrs Brown: "Yes, we _____ (to book) a holiday in Canada three months ago and _____ (to pick up) the tickets from the travel agent four weeks later.

But we _____ (to have not got) any Canadian money yet."

Bank manager: "_____ you _____ (to decide) how much you need?"

Mrs Brown: "We _____ (to talk) about that yesterday and we need 5,000 Canadian dollars."

Bank manager: "_____ you _____ (to phone) us yesterday?"

Mr Brown: "Yes, we _____ (to call) in the afternoon."

Bank manager: "The money _____ (not to come)

4 Die Zeitformen des Verbs

from the main bank yet." Mrs Brown: "That's not good."

Bank manager: "Wait a minute. I _____ (to check) an

hour ago but perhaps it _____ (to come) since then."

Bank manager: "A man _____ just _____ (to bring)

the money from the main bank. It is here."

Mr Brown: "We _____ (not to ask) yet how much a

Canadian dollar is."

Bank manager: "I _____ (to check) yesterday

and 5,000 dollars _____ (to be) 2,500 pounds. But I

_____ (not to look) today yet. But I think it's the same." |15|

★ ❷ **Bilde ganze Sätze aus den angegebenen Satzteilen. Benutze das *present perfect* oder das *simple past*.**

1. I / to meet / Peter / two years ago

   _____

2. he / to be / a good friend / ever since

   _____

3. I / to meet / him / last Saturday

   _____

4. he / not to phone / me / yet

   _____

pro richtige Zeit 1 Punkt; pro richtige Wortstellung 1 Punkt |8|

mixed tenses

1 Lauren hat nächste Woche Geburtstag und denkt darüber nach.
Ergänze in dem Text die Verben in Klammern in der richtigen Zeit: *simple present, will-future, going to-future, simple past* oder *present perfect*.

1. What _____ I _____ (to get) for my 12th birthday next week?

2. I hope this year I _____ (to get) what I really need.

3. Last year I _____ (to need) a pair of boots,

    but Mum _____ (to buy) me a new pair of shoes.

4. And I _____ (to want) a computer, but Dad

    _____ (to give) me a new bicycle.

5. Every year I _____ (to tell) him my birthday wishes,

    and he always _____ (to forget) them.

6. That _____ (not to be) very funny.

7. I _____ (not to want) any presents that I

    _____ (not to like).

8. I _____ (to need) some new T-shirts every year.

9. Mum always _____ (to buy) me a new sweatshirt.

10. Perhaps I _____ (to get) a new pair of jeans next week.

11. I hope Mum _____ (to buy) a new skirt for me, too.

12. I think I _____ (to get) some money from my Grandma

    for my birthday.

13. I _____ (to buy) a new pair of basketball trainers then.

4 Die Zeitformen des Verbs

2 Ergänze in dem Text die Verben in Klammern in der richtigen Zeit: *simple present, will-future, going to-future, simple past* oder *present perfect*.

One week after her birthday, Lauren wants to buy a new pair of basketball trainers in a sports shop.

1. Shop assistant: "Good afternoon. Can I _____ (to help) you?"

2. Lauren: "I _____ (to need) a new pair of trainers.

   But I _____ (not to decide) yet."

3. Shop assistant: "What size* _____ you _____ (to take)?"

4. Lauren: "Normally I _____ (to take) size 5."

5. Shop assistant: "_____ you ever _____ (to have) a pair

   of Pike trainers?"

6. Lauren: "No, I _____ (not to have)."

7. Shop assistant: "Last week we _____ (to get) the new collection**

   of trainers. They _____ (to be) very comfortable. I think

   I _____ (to go) and get you a pair of Pike trainers in size 5."

8. Lauren: "I _____ (not to like) the colour.

   I _____ (to buy) a nice pair of trainers here last year."

9. Shop assistant: "Let me see. Yes, the Lions trainers. But I _____

   (to be) sorry. We _____ (not to have got) them any more.

   Perhaps we _____ (to get) some new ones next week."

10. Lauren: "OK, perhaps I _____ (to come) back next week."

* size = Größe ** new collection = die neuen Modelle

|16|

57

  33 – 28 Punkte  27 – 18 Punkte  17 – 0 Punkte Gesamtpunktzahl

mixed tenses – Fragen

1 Unterstreiche in dem folgenden Zeitungsartikel alle Verben im *simple past*.

Jamie wrote an article about a traffic accident for the Nottingham High School school magazine:

An accident

On August 28th, Susan, an 11-year-old girl, went by bike down the High Street. She was very fast on her new mountain bike. Suddenly a boy on his skateboard crossed the street. Susan and the boy crashed into one another. Susan broke her right arm and the boy sprained* his foot and had a big bump on his head. The boy's name is Chris and he's 11, too. Susan and Chris both go to Nottingham High School. They are in the same class and they are friends.
An ambulance took Susan and Chris to hospital where a doctor x-rayed** Susan's arm and Chris's foot.

They did not go to school for one week. Susan read a lot of comics and Chris played computer games every day. He got a new game for Christmas.
Chris liked it at home with his new computer game. This was his first accident. He loved having one week with no school.
Susan was very unhappy at home because it was her second accident this year. In February she had an accident with her bike, too, because the roads were wet and she couldn't brake***.
So, kids, be careful when you cross the street! And don't speed on your mountain bikes!

* to sprain = verstauchen ** to x-ray = röntgen *** to brake = bremsen

21

Before Jamie wrote the article, he went to Susan's house and asked her a lot of questions.

★ **2** Lies Susans Antworten und schreibe dann die Fragen auf, die Jamie gestellt hat. Falls ein Satzteil unterstrichen ist, musst du auch das richtige Fragewort finden.

1. Jamie: *"Did you go by bike?"*

   Susan: "Yes, I went by bike."

58

4 Die Zeitformen des Verbs

2. Jamie: "_____?"

   Susan: "Yes, I rode very fast on my mountain bike."

3. Jamie: "_____?"

   Susan: "Yes, the boy on the skateboard crossed the street."

4. Jamie: "_____?"

   Susan: "Yes, we have been in the same class for a long time."

5. Jamie: "_____?"

   Susan: "Yes, we are friends."

6. Jamie: "_____?"

   Susan: "The ambulance took us to <u>hospital</u>."

7. Jamie: "_____?"

   Susan: "The doctor <u>x-rayed my arm and Chris's foot</u>.

8. Jamie: "_____?"

   Susan: "I had my first accident in <u>February</u>."

9. Jamie: "What about Chris? _____ ever _____ before?"

   Susan: "No, he has never had an accident before."

10. Jamie: "_____?"

    Susan: "No, I will not go to school tomorrow."

    Jamie: "Thank you, Susan. I hope you get well soon."

pro richtige Frage 2 Punkte   18

Wortstellung

Du kannst dich bestimmt noch erinnern: In englischen **Aussagesätzen** ist die **Wortstellung** *(word order)* anders als in deutschen, nämlich:
Subjekt – Prädikat – Objekt – Ortsangaben – Zeitangaben.
Bei anderen Satzarten können die Satzteile an anderer Position stehen.

1 Schreibe die angegebenen Satzteile in der richtigen Satzstellung auf. Denke an die Großschreibung am Satzanfang.

1. to your friends / want to send / do / a letter / you / for Christmas?

   Do you want to send a letter to your friends for Christmas?

2. of December / your letters / should send / you / at the beginning

   _____

3. on the front of / the address / should write / you / the envelope

   _____

4. the stamp / don't forget / in the right corner / to put

   _____

5. want to send / by airmail? / do / it / you

   _____

6. an airmail sticker / put / then / on the envelope

   _____

7. to put / do not / into the postbox / the letter / forget

   _____

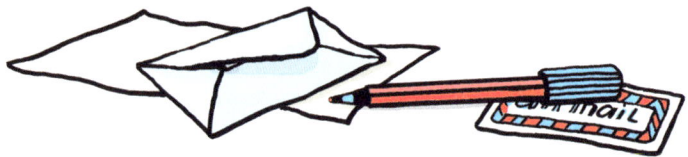

5 Der Satz

2 Ben will Postkarten verschicken. Trage die Satzteile unten in der richtigen Satzstellung und an der richtigen Stelle des Gesprächs zwischen Ben und dem Postangestellten ein.
Denke an die Großschreibung am Satzanfang.

- [ ] very / you / thank / much.
- [1] to Germany? / a postcard / how much / is
- [ ] for postcards / need / I / 10 stamps / to Germany
- [ ] and / need / for a postcard / I / one stamp / to the USA
- [ ] please? / can / put on / the airmail sticker / you / for me
- [ ] to send / I'd like / it / by airmail / yes
- [ ] any nice stamps? / have / got / you   [6]

1. Ben: *"How much is a postcard to Germany?"*

   Post office clerk: "It's 56p."

2. Ben: "_____."

3. Ben: "_____."

   Post office clerk: "Here are ten stamps for the postcards to Germany. Do you want to send the postcard to the USA by airmail?"

4. Ben: "_____."

5. Ben: "_____?"

   Post office clerk: "Yes, I have. You need an airmail sticker, too."

6. Ben: "_____?"

   Post office clerk: "Yes, of course."

7. Ben: "_____." [6]

Vermischte Übungen

Hier kannst du überprüfen, was du schon kannst.
Tipp: Wenn du unsicher bist, schau auf den in Klammern angegebenen Seiten nach.

1 Frage nach den hervorgehobenen Satzteilen. Benutze die Fragewörter *where*, *when* und *what*. Schreibe die Fragen in der richtigen Zeit über die Antworten. (Seite 24–25, 40–41, 58–59)

1. _____?

   Mr Brown works in the garden on Saturday afternoons.

2. _____?

   She bought a packet of biscuits.

3. _____?

   The Millers always get up at seven o'clock.

4. _____?

   The children never play football in the street.

pro richtiges Fragewort 1 Punkt [4]
pro richtige Zeit 1 Punkt [4]

2 *Will-* oder *going to-future*? Schreibe die Verben in Klammern in der richtigen Zeit in die Lücken. (Seite 42–47)

1. I think he _____ (to be) 13 next year.

2. Hurry up! The film _____ (to start) in a few seconds!

3. They _____ (to play) football after school.

4. Look at the clouds! It _____ (to rain).

[4]

5 Der Satz

3 Streiche die falsche Zeitform durch. (Seite 46–47, 54–55)

1. I think it is going to rain / will rain.
2. She bought / has bought a new dress yesterday.
3. I haven't done / didn't do my homework yet.

4 Bilde mit den angegebenen Satzteilen einen Aussagesatz (✓), einen Negativsatz (✗) oder eine Frage (?) im *present perfect*. (Seite 48–53)

1. Peter / just / to do / his homework (✓)

   _____

2. the boys / to go / shopping / yet (?)

   _____

3. John / to buy / a new exercise book / yet (✗)

   _____

5 *Present perfect* oder *simple past*? Schreibe die Verben in Klammern in der richtigen Zeitform in die Lücken. (Seite 54–55)

On my way home yesterday I _____ (to see) a big black car.

I thought: "I _____ (not to see) that car in our street

before." I _____ (to ask) my father but he _____

(not to know) the car. So we _____ (to call) the police.

They _____ (to come) at once. "How often _____ you

_____ (to see) that car?" _____ (to ask) a policeman.

"Twice," I _____ (to say). "Well, somebody _____ (to steal)

this car last week."

Autorinnen Ingrid Preedy und Brigitte Seidl

Bibliografische Information der Deutschen Nationalbibliothek
Die Deutsche Nationalbibliothek verzeichnet diese Publikation in der
Deutschen Nationalbibliografie; detaillierte bibliografische Daten sind
im Internet über http://dnb.dnb.de abrufbar.

Das Wort **Duden** ist für den Verlag Bibliographisches Institut GmbH als Marke
geschützt.

Kein Teil dieses Werkes darf ohne schriftliche Einwilligung des Verlages in irgendeiner
Form (Fotokopie, Mikrofilm oder ein anderes Verfahren), auch nicht für Zwecke der
Unterrichtsgestaltung, reproduziert oder unter Verwendung elektronischer Systeme
verarbeitet, vervielfältigt oder verbreitet werden.

Alle Rechte vorbehalten.
Nachdruck, auch auszugsweise, nicht gestattet.

1. Auflage
© Duden 2013   J I H
Bibliographisches Institut GmbH
Mecklenburgische Straße 53, 14197 Berlin

Redaktionelle Leitung Anika Donner, Heike Gras
Redaktion Marion Krause
Illustrationen Dorina Tessmann
Herstellung Ursula Fürst
Layout Horst Bachmann
Umschlaggestaltung 2issue, München
Umschlagillustration Dorina Tessmann
Satz Satzpunkt Ursula Ewert GmbH, Bayreuth
Druck und Bindung AZ Druck und Datentechnik GmbH, Heisinger Straße 16, 87437 Kempten

Printed in Germany

ISBN 978-3-411-87139-1

PEFC zertifiziert
Dieses Produkt stammt aus nachhaltig
bewirtschafteten Wäldern und kontrollierten
Quellen.

www.pefc.de

PEFC/04-31-2260